SHEFFIELD
THEN & NOW

IN COLOUR

GEOFFREY HOWSE

The History Press

This book is dedicated to the memory of my aunt
Joan Bostwick
1928–2010

First published in hardback 2011, this paperback edition 2015

The History Press
The Mill, Brimscombe Port
Stroud, Gloucestershire, GL5 2QG
www.thehistorypress.co.uk

British Library Cataloguing in Publication Data.
A catalogue record for this book is available from the British Library.

ISBN 978 0 7509 6499 9

Typesetting and origination by The History Press
Printed in China

CONTENTS

ACKNOWLEDGEMENTS

Iris Ackroyd, Mary Ackroyd, Stuart Ackroyd, Victoria Ackroyd, Jessica Andrews, Keith Atack, Vera Atack, Keith Bamforth, Marlene Bamforth, Michael Barber, Susan Barber, Caroline Bostwick, Daniel Bostwick, Fay Bostwick, Josh Bostwick, Laura Bostwick, Luke Bostwick, Neil Bostwick, Paul Bostwick, Sue Bostwick, Tony Briggs, Liz Burgess, Robert Burgess, Kathleen Dale, Robert A. Dale, Iris Deller, Joanna C. Murray Deller, Ricky S. Deller, Tracy P. Deller, Christine Dulson, Gary Dulson, Angela Elliott, Brian Elliott, Joyce Finney, David Greenfield, Pamela Greenfield, George Hardy, Sue Harrison of Weston Park Museum, Elaine Hickman, Steven Hickman, Ann Howse, Doreen Howse, Kathleen Howse, Raymond Mellor Jones, Alan Liptrot, Kristin Liptrot, Christine Johnson, Martyn Johnson, Michael Lambert, Doug McHale, Yvonne McHale, Bob Mortimer, Graham Noble, Tom Noble, Vale Noble, Barbara Nelder, Eleanor Nelder, Stanley Nelder, Terry Nelder, Anthony Richards, David J. Richardson, Lindy Stevenson, Michelle Tilling, Rose Vickers, Adam R. Walker, Anna Walker, Arthur O. Walker, Christine Walker, Darren J. Walker, Emma C. Walker, Ivan P. Walker, Jenny Walker, Paula L. Walker, Suki B. Walker, Thomas A. Walker, Walkers Newsagents (Hoyland), Clifford Willoughby, Margaret Willoughby, Betty Young, Roy Young, I would also like to thank John D. Murray who has assisted me over many years; and finally, not forgetting my ever-faithful walking companion, Coco.

ABOUT THE AUTHOR

Geoffrey Howse, actor, author and historian, was born in Sheffield. He has become well known for his books and writing about Yorkshire subjects, including *A Century of Sheffield*, *Images of Sheffield*, *A Photographic History of Sheffield Steel*, *Foul Deeds & Suspicious Deaths in & Around Sheffield*, *Doncaster Past & Present*, *Around Hoyland*, *Foul Deeds & Suspicious Deaths in & Around Barnsley*, *Foul Deeds & Suspicious Deaths in South Yorkshire*, *The Wentworths of Wentworth & The Fitzwilliam (Wentworth) Estates*, and *The Little Book of Yorkshire*. His other books include: *Foul Deeds & Suspicious Deaths in London's East End*, *Foul Deeds & Suspicious Deaths in London's West End*, *North London Murders*, *The A–Z of London Murders* and *Murder & Mayhem in North London*.

INTRODUCTION

Sheffield's origins are linked to a site high above the River Don, where the remains of an Iron Age hill fort occupy a commanding position on Wincobank Hill, built to defend the local population. The Celts, Vikings and Anglo Saxons left behind them a legacy, which is recalled in many of the local names. The first mention of Sheffield is in the Domesday Survey of 1086, when it is spelt in three different ways: Scafeld, Escafeld, and Sceult. Although the Anglo Saxon lords exerted some influence in the area that slowly grew into the town of Sheffield, it was the Norman Lord William de Lovetot who built a castle there during the twelfth century and who in all probability founded the town of Sheffield proper, which grew alongside and around his residence.

Sheffield has been a city since 1893, its parish church being raised to cathedral status in 1914. It was built on seven hills and five river valleys, the rivers being the Sheaf (from which Sheffield took its name, meaning the 'open country by the Sheaf'), Don, Porter, Loxley and Rivelin. Its rivers played an important part in the development of the industries for which Sheffield has become world-renowned, the production of cutlery and steel.

It was really the close proximity of plentiful supplies of water and the rich beds of iron ore that were responsible for the growth of the iron and steel industry in Sheffield. Early industry was quick to make use of the rivers as a source of power. Timber was readily available and this was turned into charcoal for the smelting and forging industries. Coal provided energy during the Industrial Revolution but it was water power that made Sheffield famous for cutlery production.

The once magnificent castle was destroyed in the aftermath of the Civil War and, apart from a few foundation stones beneath the current Castle Market, nothing remains. After the arrest of Mary Queen of Scots in 1569, Queen Elizabeth I appointed her loyal subject George, 6th Earl of Shrewsbury, as her custodian. The Queen of Scots was brought to Sheffield and remained in his charge from 1570 to 1584, mainly imprisoned at Sheffield Castle and Sheffield Manor Lodge, Lord Shrewsbury's two fine residences there.

Today, Sheffield, as well as having become a renowned centre of learning, with two universities, has become known as a city of sport. It already had an enviable record in staging events before the Sports Council named it Britain's First National City of Sport in 1995. Soccer was born in Sheffield. Sheffield FC, founded on 24 October 1857, is the world's oldest football club and produced the first soccer rule book at a time when the area had fifteen teams. In 1877 an agreement was made between the London Association and the Sheffield Association to use the same rules, which formed the basis of the rules still in use today.

I have chosen a selection of images of old Sheffield, some dating back more than 130 years, showing several of the city's architecturally important or popular features, which have long since disappeared. Some were completely obliterated in December 1940 during the Sheffield Blitz. Others were demolished during the creation of new thoroughfares, such as Arundel Gate and Furnival Gate. There have been some splendid additions to Sheffield's great architectural heritage in recent years. The modern views, showing the same locations as those in the old photographs and taken from the same spots, clearly illustrate just how dramatic the changes to Sheffield have been.

Geoffrey Howse, 2011

ST PETER'S CHURCH

A LATE NINETEENTH-CENTURY view of St Peter's church, Sheffield's parish church. Most of the old cruciform church dates from the first half of the fifteenth century, although there are older

fragments, including good stained glass and part of a fourteenth-century Jesse window. The Shrewsbury Chapel, built c.1520, contains important tombs of the earls of Shrewbury, owners of Sheffield Castle and Sheffield Manor Lodge. Raised to cathedral status in 1914, the former parish church is now known as the Cathedral Church of St Peter and St Paul. On the right of the churchyard is Parade Chambers, which contains a profusion of decorative stone carvings by Frank Tory, including a panel with the sculpted heads of Geoffrey Chaucer and William Caxton. Frank Tory's twin sons Alfred and William trained under their father, and many of Sheffield's finest buildings are greatly enhanced by their work.

THE CATHEDRAL CHURCH of St Peter and St Paul, pictured above on a cold winter morning in January 2011. In 1919, Sir Charles Nicholson was engaged to transform the old parish church into a building more befitting its cathedral status, and in April 1937, a massive programme of work was implemented, continuing until 1942. Following a further building programme, The Chapel of The Holy Spirit was dedicated in 1948. Sir Charles Nicholson's successor Steven Dykes Bower continued to build and was joined in 1956 by George Pace. However, both resigned because their work was hindered by costs. The work was eventually completed by Arthur Bailey, and some of the exterior additions are clearly visible in the present day. On the right, part of Parade Chambers, Pawson and Brailsford's former premises at No. 1 High Street, is occupied by Lloyds TSB Bank.

CHURCH STREET

CHURCH STREET, 1903. The carriages and cabs on the left are parked outside St Peter's church. On the right is the Cutlers' Hall, the home of the Cutlers' Company in Hallamshire. This comparatively modest Church Street façade masks a complex and extensive arrangement

of rooms. The Cutlers' Hall is the setting for the annual celebration of Sheffield's manufacturing industry, the Cutlers' Feast, which enables those with local business interests to meet and influence the wider political and commercial community. To the left is the Royal Bank of Scotland, designed in a mid-Victorian interpretation of the palazzo style, beyond which is Cole Brothers' department store.
(Reproduced with kind permission of David J. Richardson)

ONE OF SHEFFIELD'S Supertrams passes through Church Street on a gloomy morning in January 2011 (above). In 1985 permission was granted to build a light tram rail system in Sheffield. The system was built by the South Yorkshire Passenger Transport Executive at a cost of £240 million and opened in stages between 1994 and 1995, the Supertram making its first journey through Sheffield's streets in May 1994. With the exception of an attic storey added by Alfred E. Turner in 1928, the Cutlers' Hall has remained unchanged in external appearance in the 108 years that have elapsed since the previous image was taken, as has Flockton & Abbot's Church Street branch of the Royal Bank of Scotland. Beyond can be seen the second building to have stood on the site of Cole Brothers' former premises since 1963, which includes an armed forces recruitment office. Next door is a branch of HSBC.

COLE'S CORNER

COLE'S CORNER IN 1963 (opposite). The popular department store Cole Brothers Ltd was founded by three brothers in 1847. The building seen here was constructed in the 1860s, and Cole's Corner became a popular meeting place. In 1963 Cole Brothers moved to new premises in Barker's Pool, after which their old store was demolished.
(Reproduced with kind permission of David J. Richardson)

THE SITE OF Cole Brothers' former store is pictured below in 2011. This is the second building to be built on the site of Cole Brothers' old store since the building was demolished following Cole Brothers' relocation to Barker's Pool in 1963. Ground floor accommodation is occupied by several shop units, with office accommodation being provided on the four floors above. The corner building, No. 2 Fargate, which fronts onto both Fargate and Church Street, is occupied by HSBC. Some Sheffielders still refer to the area as Cole's Corner.

COLE'S CORNER AND FARGATE

COLE'S CORNER AND Fargate seen from the junction of High Street and Church Street shortly before the First World War. Two of Sheffield's trams can be seen travelling along Fargate. The first tramway line, a horse-drawn service, started in 1875 when a line opened between Lady's Bridge and Attercliffe. In 1899, the first electric tram ran between Nether Edge and Tinsley. The last trams ran between Leopold Street and Beauchief on 8 October 1960.

A VIEW OF Fargate taken from the same spot in 2011 (above). The imposing building in the left foreground was designed as an auction house by Flockton & Gibbs. Barclays Bank occupied the premises for many years until after the turn of the twenty-first century. In January 2011 the premises are occupied by Café Nero. Next door, No. 9 Fargate is in fact deceptively large, extending backwards; plots such as these reflect the width of plots of some of Fargate's ancient buildings. Black Swan Walk runs from Fargate down the left-hand side of No. 9 and Chapel Walk runs down the right-hand side. The building was formerly the premises of A.H. Holland, who had a say in its design. A great lover of art, he was heavily influenced by John Ruskin and William Morris. During Holland's occupancy, part of the building was given over to the display of paintings and fine pottery. The premises are currently occupied by Virgin Media. The utilitarian modernist buildings seen beyond the opening to Chapel Walk on the east side of Fargate contain shops and offices but are of little architectural importance. Across the road, out of sight in this view, however, are some important survivals.

FARGATE FROM
PINFOLD STREET

THIS PRE-1900 POSTCARD (right) showing Fargate was
taken from Pinfold Street. Fargate is at the heart of Sheffield's
commercial and retail quarter. Its name is derived from the Old
Norse word *gata*, meaning a street or lane. The prefix 'far' may
indicate that this once marked the furthest extension of the old
town from the castle, where the town had its origins in the twelfth
century. The Albany Hotel on the right was built in 1888–89 for
the Yorkshire Penny Bank. The obelisk on the left is the Jubilee
Memorial, erected in 1887, which bears the inscription:

ERECTED TO COMMEMORATE THE JUBILEE OF QUEEN VICTORIA, 1887

The obelisk was moved to Endcliffe Park in 1905 and replaced by a statue of Queen Victoria by Alfred Turner.

A NOW PEDESTRIANISED Fargate viewed from Pinfold Street in January 2011 (left). The building in the left foreground contains the entrance to Orchard Square, a popular and architecturally pleasing shopping area, which successfully combines old and new buildings. Next door stands the 1902 former National Provincial Bank. A few buildings further along is J.D. Webster's late Gothic-style retail premises, built for provision merchants Arthur Davy in 1881–82 and claimed to be the largest provision store in the country. Distinctive carvings above the third floor show the heads of a sheep, cow, pig and ox, proclaiming the potted meat, pies and hams for which Davy's was noted. The premises are currently occupied by W.H. Smith. The large building on the right is still occupied by the bank, but the Albany Hotel is no more. The building has been much altered: the gabled dormers, crenellated parapet and chimneys disappeared during the building's conversion from hotel to offices towards the end of the 1960s and the original red brick façade was faced with stone.

FARGATE FROM TOWN HALL SQUARE

A 1907 VIEW (left) of Fargate taken from Town Hall Square. The approximately 10ft-high statue of Queen Victoria is of bronze and stands on top of a plinth of limestone blocks. It bears the date 1904, although it was not put in place until the following year. The statue was unveiled by Princess Beatrice of Battenberg on 11 May 1905. On one side of the stone plinth are bronze figures representing 'Maternity': a young woman holds a baby and her left arm is draped around the shoulders of a little girl. On the other side is the bronze figure representing 'Labour': a young man, with shirt sleeves rolled up, sits on an anvil with a sledgehammer resting against his left inner leg. The statue remained *in situ* until 1930 when it was moved to Endcliffe Park.

FARGATE VIEWED FROM Town Hall Square in January 2011 (above). On the left is the arched arcaded entrance to Orchard Square, part of Chapman Taylor Partners' extensive 1987 building scheme. Many of Fargate's Victorian buildings remain but others, like some of those on the right, have been in-filled by more recent and, sadly, sometimes architecturally unsympathetic modern buildings. At the far end of Fargate across High Street can be seen the white clock tower of the 1913 *Sheffield Telegraph* building.

FARGATE

A PRE-FIRST WORLD War postcard view of Fargate. The late Gothic building to the left of the Yorkshire Penny Bank, on the east side of Fargate, which curves round into Norfolk Row, was built

in 1889–92 by H.W. Lockwood for the YMCA. There are carvings by Frank Tory, including six arched panels depicting the days of Creation and four showing the progress of Divine Law.

TODAY'S FARGATE REMAINS a busy shopping area. Since the street became pedestrianised there are numerous benches to stop for a rest or to have a drink from one of the many take-away outlets. Street musicians and other performers have become regular features of this thoroughfare, as have the ubiquitous vendors of the *Big Issue* and charity canvassers. Always popular with Sheffielders and visitors alike, Fargate has managed to retain many well-known, long established high street names, as well as attracting new national chain stores.

FARGATE, EAST SIDE

THE EAST SIDE of Fargate, 1920 (left). Hanbidge's shop is at the junction of Norfolk Row.
(Reproduced with kind permission of David J. Richardson)

THE EAST SIDE of Fargate, seen above in January 2011. Considerable changes have taken place in the ninety-one years that have elapsed between the two photographs. The premises occupied by costumier and silk specialists H.E. Closs & Co. Ltd at No. 37 Fargate in 1920 is now a branch of the travel agent Thomas Cook and is the only building to have survived. Marks & Spencer can be seen on the left and other well-known outlets, such as Dorothy Perkins and Topman, have become well established. The tower of the Roman Catholic Cathedral Church of St Marie, situated in Norfolk Row, can be seen on the right.

THE GOODWIN FOUNTAIN

GOODWIN FOUNTAIN, SEEN opposite during the 1960s. The fountain was dedicated to Sir Stuart and Lady Goodwin. Sir Stuart was an alderman, benefactor of many local charities and a prominent Sheffield steel magnate who founded the Neepsend Tool and Steel Corporation. The fountain seen here occupied the site from 1961–98, when it was replaced by a new fountain located in the Peace Gardens. Yorkshire House, the elegant building with pedimented entrance, columns and pilasters seen behind the Goodwin Fountain is occupied by Wilson Peck,

the music store, situated at the corner of Leopold Street and Barkers Pool. The building was designed by Flockton & Gibbs in 1883–34. The top floor and attic were added in 1892. Barker's Pool dates back as far as 1435, when a Mr Barker built an enclosed reservoir, which existed until 1793.

A 2011 VIEW across the end of Fargate, which shows the site of former landmarks including the Jubilee Memorial, Alfred Turner's statue of Queen Victoria and the Goodwin Fountain. The one-time music store in Yorkshire House, which straddles Barker's Pool and Leopold Street, is now occupied by H.L. Brown, jewellers, and the Yorkshire Building Society.

HIGH STREET FROM FARGATE

HIGH STREET VIEWED from the corner of Fargate in the 1890s (left). One of Sheffield's oldest streets, High Street was originally a link between the medieval castle and the parish church. Parts of the old High Street were only 20ft wide. In the closing years of the nineteenth century, street widening began and many buildings were demolished. W. Foster & Son, whose advertising sign boasts that they are the 'Oldest Clothiers in the City', is at No. 8 High Street and W. Lewis's tobacconists is at No. 6. Not long after this photograph was taken many of the buildings seen here were torn down to facilitate the widening of High Street.
(Reproduced with kind permission of David J. Richardson)

SHOP UNITS IN High Street today are occupied by nationally known chains, such as Boots the chemists, HMV and Primark.

HIGH STREET

AN EARLY EDWARDIAN postcard (right) featuring a substantially rebuilt High Street. The buildings on the right (south side) have been set back in the extensive rebuilding programme that had recently been undertaken. The Huddersfield stone Fosters' Buildings of 1896 were designed in a French domestic Gothic style by Flockton, Gibbs & Flockton. Fosters, the gentlemen's outfitters, continued to occupy trading premises. The building also incorporated Sheffield's first American elevator. Many buildings in High Street were completely destroyed or damaged beyond reasonable repair during the Sheffield Blitz in December 1940.

HIGH STREET IN 2011 (left). Parade Chambers at No. 1 High Street can be seen on the left. Modern buildings occupy the sites where more elegant structures once stood, before they were damaged in the Sheffield Blitz. Fosters' Buildings, in the right foreground, sustained only slight damage during the bombing raids and survived to enhance High Street's appearance in the twenty-first century.

HIGH STREET FROM COLE'S CORNER

A 1940s POSTCARD view (right) of High Street taken from Cole's Corner at the junction with Fargate. More demolition and rebuilding has taken place, with the white faience *Sheffield Telegraph* building, Kemsley House (on the north side, constructed in 1913–16 and designed by Gibbs, Flockton and Teather), being the most notable example of a major change to the streetscape. It is a

striking building with Baroque details, a corner domed entrance and a five-bay south front with two tiers of giant arched window openings and a glazed central square clock tower with a dome.

KEMSLEY HOUSE IS now occupied by Santander Bank. On the south side of High Street, bomb-damaged buildings have been replaced by less architecturally sophisticated shops and offices.

FITZALAN MARKET

FITZALAN MARKET, 1905. Situated at the top of Angel Street on the corner of High Street, the area to the front of the building on the Angel Street side was known as Market Place. The horse and cart is crossing High Street from Fitzalan Square. Fitzalan Market opened in 1786, but the building which replaced the original, seen here, dates from 1864.
(Reproduced with kind permission of David J. Richardson)

A 2011 VIEW (above) from the junction of High Street and Angel across Castle Square. Primark have taken over the building previously occupied by C&A, which replaced the Blitz-damaged Burton Building, itself built on the site of the demolished Fitzalan Market. Panache House (the Early Renaissance palazzo-style offices built for the Sheffield United Gas Light Co. in Commercial Street, 1874, by M.E. Hadfield & Son) can be seen to the left behind the bus.

HIGH STREET FROM ANGEL STREET

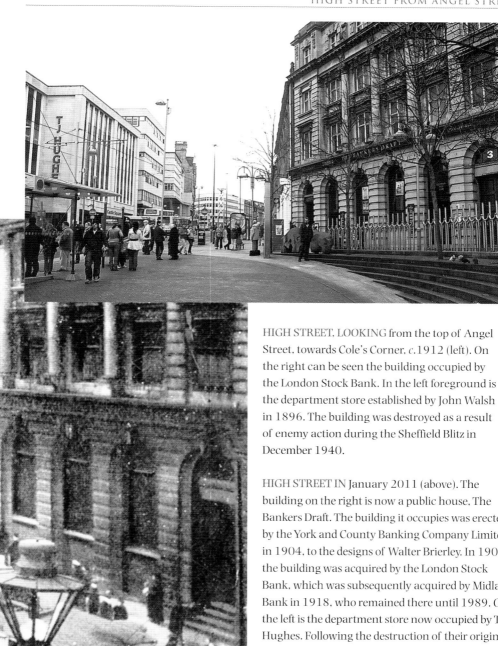

HIGH STREET, LOOKING from the top of Angel Street, towards Cole's Corner, *c.*1912 (left). On the right can be seen the building occupied by the London Stock Bank. In the left foreground is the department store established by John Walsh in 1896. The building was destroyed as a result of enemy action during the Sheffield Blitz in December 1940.

HIGH STREET IN January 2011 (above). The building on the right is now a public house, The Bankers Draft. The building it occupies was erected by the York and County Banking Company Limited in 1904, to the designs of Walter Brierley. In 1909 the building was acquired by the London Stock Bank, which was subsequently acquired by Midland Bank in 1918, who remained there until 1989. On the left is the department store now occupied by T.J. Hughes. Following the destruction of their original store, Walsh's traded elsewhere in Sheffield until a new store, built to the designs of J.S. Beaumont, opened on the site of their bombed premises. In the 1970s Walsh's became Rackhams' and, in the 1980s, House of Fraser. After the store's closure in 1998 the premises were taken over by T.J. Hughes.

HIGH STREET FROM
COMMERCIAL STREET

HIGH STREET FROM the junction of Commercial Street with Fitzalan Square in the 1930s (left). The clock tower of Kemsley House, with its distinctive dome and the spire of the Cathedral Church of St Peter and St Paul, can be seen in the centre background. On the right, at the corner of Angel Street, the Burton Building stands on the site of the former Fitzalan Market.

A 2011 VIEW (above) from the same spot as the previous image. Sheffield Blitz-damaged buildings at the eastern end of High Street have been replaced by the buildings seen here.

PINSTONE STREET

AN EARLY EDWARDIAN postcard view of Pinstone Street and Town Hall Square, looking across the edge of Barker's Pool into Leopold Street. The postcard is franked 29 May 1905. Occupying Nos. 30–42 is a building containing shops and offices, with flats above, with a frontage of fifteen bays. It was built in two phases, 1893–94 and 1896, of red brick with stone dressings and cast iron balconies, by Reuben Thompson, a horse bus and coach and

cab proprietor. Beyond is Palatine Chambers, built to the design of Flockton & Gibbs in 1895. The curved front of Yorkshire House can be seen at the corner of Barker's Pool and Leopold Street.

PINSTONE STREET IN January 2011 (above). On the west side of the street the first group of buildings are shops and offices forming part of the development built to the designs of William Gilbee Scott in 1892 for the Salvation Army. Beyond is Reuben Thompson's building and Palatine Chambers, which was remodelled in the 1970s. In the centre background at the corner of Leopold Street can be seen part of Chapman Taylor Partners' 1987 Orchard Square development.

37

ST PAUL'S CHURCH AND THE TOWN HALL

THIS LATE NINETEENTH-CENTURY postcard shows St Paul's church in all its magnificence and beyond it Sheffield's newly built town hall. The Jubilee Memorial can just be glimpsed in the bottom left-hand corner, and the spire of St Marie's church can be seen above the roof of St Paul's. After the raising of the parish church to cathedral status in 1914, and owing to a shift of population

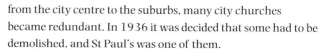

from the city centre to the suburbs, many city churches became redundant. In 1936 it was decided that some had to be demolished, and St Paul's was one of them.

THE SITE OF the demolished St Paul's church in January 2011 is pictured above. The old town hall had served Sheffield since 1808, but with an ever-increasing population, facilities in Waingate became inadequate. Following Sheffield being granted a City Charter in 1893, it was decided that a larger and grander building would be more appropriate, and 178 architects entered the competition to design the new town hall. Constructed to the winning design by E.W. Mountford, construction began in 1891 and the new town hall was officially opened by Queen Victoria on 21 May 1897. The Peace Gardens were created in 1998 and replaced an earlier gardens opened there in 1938, commemorating the peace promised by the Munich agreement. They contain artwork by metalworker Brian Asquith, ceramicist Tracey Hayes and stone carver Richard Perry, and spectacular water features, which represent Sheffield's rivers and molten metal – the source of its power and wealth. The building to the right of the town hall is St Paul's Hotel and Spa.

MOORHEAD AND PINSTONE STREET

A C.1910 POSTCARD of Moorhead and Pinstone Street. The tower of St Paul's church can be seen in the centre of the image. The monument, surrounded by iron railings, was erected on this site in 1863 to the designs of George Goldie and commemorated servicemen who had died

in the Crimean War. Its foundation stone had been laid in 1857 by the Duke of Cambridge. The seated figure that tops the monument represents 'Honour'. The Crimean War Memorial was removed from Moorhead in 1957 and placed, minus its column, in the Botanical Gardens.

MOORHEAD AND PINSTONE Street in January 2011 can be seen above. Much of The Moor suffered severe damage during the Sheffield Blitz and most of the buildings between Moorhead and Moorfoot are modern replacements. Rebuilt during the '50s and '60s, for the most part the department stores and shop units can at best be described as functional. They are mostly faced in Portland stone, with the occasional use of marble panels. Crossing The Moor, in the foreground, is Furnival Square, named after a once prominent local family. Many of the buildings that had escaped major bomb damage around Moorhead succumbed to the ball and chain of the demolition crane during Furnival Gate's creation.

MOORHEAD

TAKEN FROM A similar spot to those in the previous two images, this 1904 photograph (right) shows the building occupied by the Public Benefit Boot Co. Ltd, which traded from these premises from 1896–1911. This famous firm traded from over 780 nationwide business premises from the 1870s to the 1970s and had several branches in Sheffield at various times, including repairing premises in Cambridge Street. On the right, across the corner of Union Street in Furnival Street, can be seen the central Sheffield offices and showrooms of the famous Sheffield firm Newton Chambers, whose steel manufacturing and construction base was at Thorncliffe, Chapeltown,

as were their chemical works. Here, amongst other notable products, the germicidal oil Izal was manufactured. The firm's showrooms, seen here, were completely gutted during the Sheffield Blitz in December 1940.
(Reproduced with kind permission of David J. Richardson)

A PRESENT DAY view (left) of Moorhead and the site of Newton Chambers' city offices and showrooms, which, although damaged by German bombs, survived until the creation of Furnival Gate.

CAMBRIDGE STREET

CAMBRIDGE STREET, SEEN here in 1926, was originally
called Coal Pit Lane as the surface working of coal once
took place in the vicinity. This street once stood at the
end of old Sheffield town and was traditionally one of
the centres of the horn- and bone-working trades, whose
finished goods were used for a variety of purposes ranging
from items manufactured in the cutlery industry to items
as diverse as snuff boxes, door knobs and drinking cups.
The street has borne its present name since 1857 when
the Duke of Cambridge laid the foundation stone for the
Crimean War Memorial at nearby Moorhead. On the left
can be seen the Hippodrome, which opened on
23 December 1907 as a variety theatre. It became a

cinema in 1931 and showed its last film, a re-screening of *Gone with the Wind*, on 2 March 1963 and was demolished shortly afterwards.
(Reproduced with kind permission of David J. Richardson)

CAMBRIDGE STREET IN 2011 (left) bears hardly any resemblance to the street seen in the 1926 image. A few of the older properties remain but the demolition and redevelopment that took place in the 1960s is clearly evident in the buildings on the left. They were constructed soon after the Hippodrome and other buildings were demolished, as part of the complex of buildings connected to the Grosvenor House Hotel. At the top of the street on the left can be seen the western side of the John Lewis department store, formerly Cole Brothers, and Sheffield City Hall, which opened in 1932, can be seen across the top of the street in Barker's Pool.

LONDON ROAD

THE BOTTOM OF London Road, *c.*1905, a somewhat dilapidated part of the new city.
(Reproduced with kind permission of David J. Richardson)

THE BOTTOM OF London Road in January 2011.
The interesting-looking building today occupied by
Sainsbury's Local began life as the Lansdowne Picture
Palace. Situated at the corner of London Road and Boston
Street, it was opened by Lansdowne Pictures Ltd in 1914.
Designed by Walter Gerard Buck, the cinema closed
following an air raid on 12 December 1940. The last film
shown there was *Vigil of the Night* with Carole Lombard
and Brian Aherne. In 1947 the building was converted
for use as a temporary Marks & Spencer. In the 1950s
it became a Mecca dance hall, the Locarno, and later
was transformed into Tiffany's nightclub before it again
reverted to its former name. During recent redevelopment
in the vicinity of London Road to provide housing and
student accommodation, the site of the auditorium has
been redeveloped, but the most distinctive part of the
former cinema has been retained.

THE CLYDE STEELWORKS

THE CLYDE STEELWORKS of Samuel Osborn & Co.
Ltd on the banks of the River Don, viewed from Blonk
Bridge, c.1900 (right). Osborn was a prominent
employer in Sheffield from 1852–1972 and moved to
the premises seen here in 1868, where they remained
until closure. The Royal Victoria Hotel, built to the
designs of M.E. Hadfield and opened in 1862, situated
in the complex adjacent to Victoria Railway Station,
can be seen on the right.

(Reproduced with kind permission of David J. Richardson)

THE RIVER DON and the site of the former steelworks of Samuel Osborn & Co. Ltd, viewed
from Blonk Bridge in January 2011 (left). The building in the left foreground provides office
accommodation, while the other buildings largely comprise riverside apartments. The Holiday Inn
Royal Victoria Hotel continues to provide accommodation for visitors to Sheffield, just as the old
hotel did during the days when the Victoria Railway Station was in its heyday. Spanning the River
Don beyond the apartment blocks on the left is Cobweb Bridge, completed in 2002 and designed
by Paul Mallinder and Richard Coe, which forms part of the Five Weirs Walk along the banks of
the river. Also known as the Spider Bridge, because large steel spiders conceal the lighting in the
ceiling, the entire structure extends beneath Wicker Arches for 100 metres.

WICKER AND WICKER ARCHES

A *c.*1907 POSTCARD of the Wicker and Wicker Arches. The wide central arch is flanked by two narrow pedestrian arches, above which are inset crests of the MS&LR, the Duke of Norfolk, the Earl of Yarborough and the Sheffield Town Trustees. The arches were constructed in 1848 by engineer John Fowler and architects Weightman & Hadfield, who were also responsible for

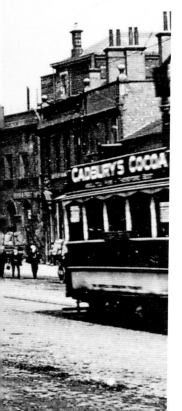

Victoria Railway Station, which can be seen on the right. The origins of the name Wicker could lie in the old Norse word *vikir*, which means willow, and *carr* or *kerr*, a broad flat meadow. The Wicker was once meadowland and lies close to the River Don which, until its banks were crowded by breweries and steelworks, may well have been fringed with willow trees.
(Reproduced with kind permission of Doreen Howse)

SEEN ABOVE IN January 2011, this part of Sheffield is no longer the bustling place it was 100 years ago. The immediate area both on and adjacent to the Wicker has been transformed, and some parts could be described as being in a state of flux. Many shops and offices have been torn down, the steelworks have long since gone and Victoria Railway Station closed on 5 January 1970. Some sites where commercial buildings once stood are now occupied by apartment blocks, breathing new life into long deserted side streets, and the general appearance of the Wicker itself has been upgraded with larger expanses of paving and stainless steel street furniture. Despite the general downturn in the Wicker's industrial fortune, its future prospects as a vibrant mix of office and living space look very promising indeed.

51

SPITAL HILL

SPITAL HILL, 1935. The twelfth-century William de Lovetot, Lord of Hallamshire, founded an isolation hospital, the Hospital of St Leonard, here. It existed until the reign of Henry VIII. Its site

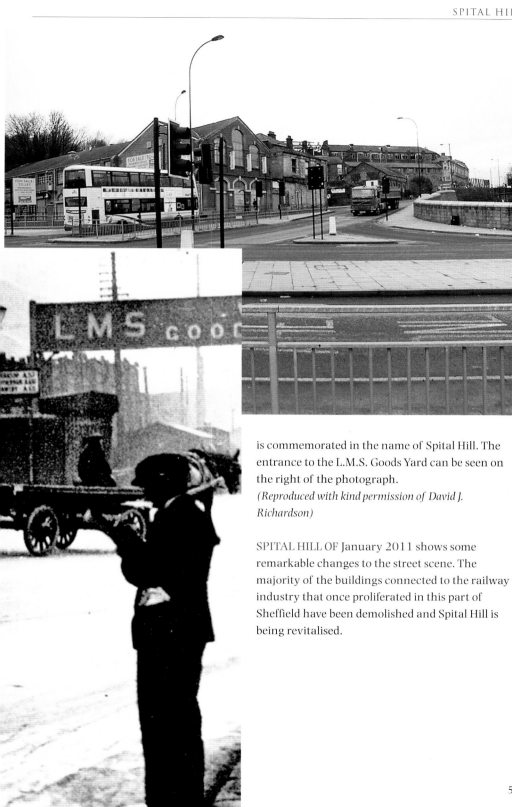

is commemorated in the name of Spital Hill. The entrance to the L.M.S. Goods Yard can be seen on the right of the photograph.
(Reproduced with kind permission of David J. Richardson)

SPITAL HILL OF January 2011 shows some remarkable changes to the street scene. The majority of the buildings connected to the railway industry that once proliferated in this part of Sheffield have been demolished and Spital Hill is being revitalised.

FURNIVAL
ROAD

THE VICTORIA HOTEL, Furnival Road, 1905 (right).
The Alexandra Theatre & Opera House, built in 1836,
can be seen on the right of the photograph. Originally
called the Adelphi, it was renamed the Alexandra Music
Hall in 1865 and was situated in Blonk Street at the
confluence of the River Sheaf and the River Don. The
stage was, reputedly, the largest in the provinces. During
its latter years, the theatre was commonly referred to
as the 'Old Alec' although for many years previously it
was popularly known as 'Tommy's' after its twice-owner
Thomas Youdan. In 1914 the theatre was purchased by
Sheffield Corporation and demolished in order to carry

out a street improvement programme. The First World War intervened. Plans were shelved and the scheme eventually went ahead in the 1930s.
(Reproduced with kind permission of David J. Richardson)

THE VIEW OPPOSITE, taken in January 2011 from the same spot as the photograph above, shows the road configuration that replaced the original layout seen in the previous image, resulting in buildings being demolished and their replacements being set back. The Alexandra Hotel is situated on a small part of the site once occupied by the Alexandra Theatre, the major portion of which stood where the bus can be seen travelling along Blonk Street.

THE CORN EXCHANGE

SHEAF STREET IN 1952, showing the Corn Exchange, built on the site of the Shrewsbury Hospital by the Duke of Norfolk in 1881. It not only provided premises for corn dealers but was

the offices of the Duke's Sheffield estates. It also contained several shop units. The building was extensively damaged by fire in 1947; it never fully reopened and only a small part of it remained in a serviceable condition. It was finally demolished in 1964.
(Reproduced with kind permission of David J. Richardson)

PARK SQUARE IN January 2011 (above). When one compares the two images on this page it seems almost incomprehensible that this was the site of the Corn Exchange, so dramatic are the changes. One of Sheffield's Supertrams can be seen passing over the square on Supertram Bridge, which was built in 1993.

LADY'S BRIDGE

LADY'S BRIDGE, PICTURED on the right in 1915, was the terminus for trams running on the Brightside and Tinsley route. A bridge has spanned the River Don at this site since 1486. The bridge gets its name from the chantry chapel, which stood on the town side, south of the present bridge until 1767. On the north side of the bridge can be seen one of the two buildings built by Flockton, Gibbs & Flockton for John Henry Bryars, an animal breeder and vet in 1899–1900. The triangular Royal Victoria Buildings had a bar and billiard and card rooms on the first floor. Its counterpart, Royal Exchange Buildings, contained twenty two-bedroom flats, as well as houses for the veterinary surgeon and groom. There was also a veterinary surgery and dogs' home plus several shops. Over the doorway to the veterinary surgery is a snake and sword, the symbols of Asclepius, the Greek god of medicine.

Built in the same style and distinctive building materials, at right angles to the back of the main
building, is Castle House, a multi-storey stables.
(Reproduced with kind permission of David J. Richardson)

ON THE LEFT on the north bank in 2011 can be seen John Henry Bryars' old premises, the
Royal Victoria Buildings, and on the right is its matching counterpart, Royal Exchange
Buildings. Castle House, the former stables, seen at the rear of Exchange Buildings, on the right
of the picture, was converted to a pioneering pea-canning factory by Chapman and Jenkinson
for Bachelors in 1931. It is now occupied by the furniture and carpet store Hancock & Lant.

THE RIVER DON

THE RIVER DON seen opposite from Blonk Bridge in 1898, at the Don's confluence with the River Sheaf. The curved building to the left of Lady's Bridge is the Lady's Bridge Hotel, built in 1852 and attached to Tennant Brothers Exchange Brewery. Industrial expansion during the early part of the nineteenth century, along with a rapidly expanding population, resulted in an enormous number of public houses – around 1,500 licensed premises according to the 1831 census. Sheffield's oldest brewery, founded in 1758, was Thos Rawson & Co. of Pond Street. To many steelworkers, the nature of their working environment meant that they were more than ready to slake their thirst with a pint or two of beer once they had finished their shift. There was a fortune to be made in the brewing industry and several large breweries were built. In 1820 Proctor & Co. established their Exchange Brewery in the Market Place, taken over twenty years later by Edward and Robert Tennant, who moved the brewery to a site adjacent to Lady's Bridge after they had sold their original premises to the Duke of Norfolk in order to build his market hall.

(Reproduced with kind permission of David J. Richardson)

A 2011 VIEW (left) of the former Lady's Bridge Hotel and Exchange Brewery (now divided into apartments and office accommodation), taken from Blonk Street Bridge. All of Sheffield's larger breweries have closed, but the tradition of brewing continues in the city at several small breweries.

FITZALAN SQUARE

AN 1890s POSTCARD featuring Fitzalan Square. This famous Sheffield square is situated at the bottom of High Street. The name is derived from a branch of the Howard family, the family name of the Dukes of Norfolk. This open space was created in 1881 on the site of buildings

which were demolished in Market Street. The Fitzalan Market can be seen across the square with Haymarket to its right. Market Street is in the left foreground.

DURING THE FIFTY-ODD years of my own lifetime I have seen many changes take place in Fitzalan Square, the majority of which, I'm sad to say, have not been to the square's betterment. I can remember this being a vibrant and thriving part of the city centre, with its proud and historic associations. Today, by comparison, Fitzalan Square appears somewhat neglected and unloved.

FITZALAN SQUARE FROM HAYMARKET

FITZALAN SQUARE VIEWED from the top of Haymarket before the First World War (right). Flat Street can be seen to the right of the general post office building, which dominates the centre background. The building with the dome in the left foreground was opened in 1881 as the Midland Banking Company. It became the United Counties bank in 1907 and was taken over by Barclays Bank in 1916. The bronze statue of His Majesty King Edward Vll dates from 1913 and is by Alfred Drury.

SEVERAL CHANGES HAVE taken place in the ninety-odd years since the photograph above was
taken. The distinctive bank building of 1881 was demolished in 1969. Walter Pott's impressive
ashlar post office building stands empty and boarded up. One notable survival can be seen on
the right. The White Building was built c.1908 by Gibbs & Flockton. Unusual at that time, it has
a faience façade by Alfred and William Tory, with ten figures in relief depicting Sheffield trades.
Standing four storeys high, with a raised attic storey, the building boasts several striking and
unusual architectural features. Next to The White Building, at the corner of Fitzalan Square in Flat
Street, can be seen the former Odeon cinema by Roger Bullivant, which was completed in 1956.

KING STREET

KING STREET FROM Market Place/Angel Street looking towards Haymarket in 1898 (left). In medieval times this street was known as Pudding Lane. Many of the buildings seen here were destroyed during Sheffield Blitz in December 1940.
(Reproduced with kind permission of David J. Richardson)

KING STREET ON a cold January afternoon in 2011 (above). The corner site with Angel Street is occupied by Castle House, the home of Sheffield Co-op. Other than the small market, whose stalls sell a variety of goods ranging from plants to pushchairs, the King Street of today is largely used by pedestrians as a shortcut from Angel Street to Waingate.

HAYMARKET

HAYMARKET, SEEN HERE in 1979 (left). This short thoroughfare runs from Fitzalan Square at the junction of Commercial Street with High Street. Haymarket becomes Waingate at Castle Street. A 'bendy bus', one of Sheffield's popular sights for over two decades, can be seen in the left foreground.
(Reproduced with kind permission of David J. Richardson)

HAYMARKET IN JANUARY 2011 (above). On the left can be seen a corner of Nos. 15–17, a late Georgian building, which was once the Brunswick public house. Until recently it had been a branch of Burger King but it is presently standing empty. The early nineteenth-century No. 19 next door is also empty and up for sale. No. 21, the 1930s building with staircase tower to the right, originally built for Arthur Davy & Sons Ltd, is occupied by Fulton Foods, a well-known Yorkshire chain. Below, Nos. 23 and 25 are early nineteenth-century houses adorned with elaborately applied half timbering. Additions were made to these in the twentieth century, which included the installation of leaded bay windows. The final building in Haymarket, whose address is actually No. 32 Castle Street, was built as a café, restaurant and shop for Arthur Davy & Sons Ltd in 1904 by Gibbs & Flockton. Part of the Castle Market complex can be seen to the right.

CASTLE MARKET

AN EARLY 1960s postcard (left) of the recently built Castle Market, seen here looking across Waingate from Castle Street. Castle Market stands on the site of Sheffield Castle, which was demolished in 1648–49 leaving hardly a trace when Parliament ordered that all castles fortified by Royalists during the Civil War should be demolished. A part of what little remains of the castle lies beneath the market complex.

A 2011 VIEW of Castle Street (above). The stone building in the left foreground is Sheffield's old town hall, which fronts onto Waingate. Sheffield's first town hall stood by the church gates in High Street. It was replaced in 1808 by the building seen here, which served as the town hall until a much larger one was opened in 1897 on a site adjacent to St Paul's church, Pinstone Street.

WAINGATE

WAINGATE, 1915 (OPPOSITE). The premises of Lenton & Rusby, who were spectacle makers and were established in Waingate in 1817, in a building opposite the town hall. They were a noted manufacturer of spectacle frames and lenses, and exported their products throughout Britain and to various European countries. The gable to the right belonged to the Royal Hotel, which opened in 1783 as the Reindeer Inn. The entire site was destroyed in December 1940 during the Sheffield Blitz.

WAINGATE IN JANUARY 2011 can be seen above. The site of Lenton & Rusby's old premises is now occupied by a branch of Dolland & Aitchison, the opticians. The shops seen here form part of the Castle Market complex.

ANGEL STREET

AN EDWARDIAN POSTCARD of Angel Street viewed from Market Place. In the right foreground at the junction of High Street is Fitzalan Market, which opened in 1786, with the original building being replaced in 1864 by the one seen here. This market specialised in meat and fish. The corn market was held each Tuesday on the High Street side. The building closed on 24 April 1930 and was demolished in 1931.

A VIEW TAKEN in January 2011, showing a transformed Angel Street. Many bomb-damaged buildings have been replaced by those seen here. On the right is Castle House, built from 1959–64 by G.S. Hay for the Brightside and Carbrook Co-operative Society as a replacement for their store in Exchange Street, which was badly damaged in the Sheffield Blitz. This large store has a highly innovative, some might say spectacular, interior. The major part of the store, just discernible in this image, lies in front of the 1962 rear extension block, seen here at the corner of King Street and constructed to the designs of Hadfield, Cawkwell & Davidson. The glass fibre figure on the wall, of Vulcan, the Roman god of fire, was created two years earlier by Boris Tietze. Long associated with Sheffield, an 8ft-tall bronze statue of Vulcan also adorns Sheffield Town Hall. Since the slimming down of the Co-operative Society in general, the premises are far less sophisticated in their presentation and are occupied by the organisation known today simply as Sheffield Co-op. Recently Castle House has been up for sale. The Co-op will continue to trade from part of the ground floor, leasing back their premises from the new owner.

COCKAYNES

COCKAYNES STORE AT 1 Angel Street, 1900 (opposite). The store was founded by two brothers, Thomas B. and William Cockayne as a general draper. The firm expanded and during the twentieth century the five-storey shop seen here was selling a wide range of goods. Cockaynes was destroyed in 1940 during the Sheffield Blitz.
(Reproduced with kind permission of David J. Richardson)

COCKAYNES BUILT A new store, which, like Walsh's new store in High Street, was designed by J.W. Beaumont & Son, in a similar style and built in 1955–56. Cockaynes traded from their new premises seen here, until they were taken over by Schofields. The entire premises are now occupied by the Argos superstore.

BIRD'S-EYE VIEW

A 1928 VIEW across the rooftops and over Midland Station to the hills beyond one of Sheffield's distinctive landmarks, the Cholera Monument, erected to the designs of M.E. Hadfield in 1834–35, which takes the form of a Gothic stone spire, standing approximately 70ft high. In the valley below amongst the many smaller factories, workshops, sawmills and steelworks are Sheaf Mills and Pond Street Brewery. In July 1832, the Asiatic Cholera epidemic struck Sheffield. Between then and November that same year, when the disease was finally brought under control,

1,347 people had been infected. Initially those who died of the disease were buried in approved churchyards, but the sheer number of deaths directly resulting from the disease led to the 12th Duke of Norfolk offering what was then a comparatively isolated site off Norfolk Road for the burial of victims of the epidemic. The disease was no respecter of class, and victims included John Blake, who was Master Cutler at the time. There are three female figures set in niches on each face of the Cholera Monument, representing 'Faith', 'Hope' and 'Charity'.
(Reproduced with kind permission of David J. Richardson)

A VIEW OF the same location (above), taken from Arundel Gate in January 2011. The changes down the hillside towards Midland Station are astounding. In 1990 the top section of the Cholera Monument was blown off during a storm. The monument underwent a complete restoration in 2005–6. The vast majority of the industrial sites that once proliferated in this part of Sheffield have gone. The building on the left is the Owen Building, now part of Sheffield Hallam University, created in 1992 from Sheffield City Polytechnic.

CENTRAL LIBRARY AND
GRAVES ART GALLERY

A 1950s VIEW of the Central Library and Graves Art Gallery in Surrey Street (left). Building began in 1929 on the site of the demolished Surrey Street Music Hall, which opened in 1823 and ended up being used as a public library. It was originally conceived as part of a never completed scheme to create a grand civic square. It was intended that the library and art gallery would form one side of this square, which would also contain civic offices, law courts and a college. The abandonment of the building of the rest of the square has left the building to appear somewhat out of kilter with its surroundings and it cannot be viewed to its full advantage from any angle, which is a pity because it is a very fine building. The Graves Art Gallery, situated on the third floor, was donated by local philanthropist Alderman J.G. Graves. His gift of almost 400 paintings and drawings formed the nucleus of the city's magnificent art collection. The Art Deco Library Theatre was built into the complex in 1934 as a lecture theatre. Dressing rooms were added in 1947, allowing the theatre to become a legitimate performance space. The buildings to the right are the Methodist Chapel and the former Surrey Street Medical School founded in 1828, which moved to Leopold Street in 1888.
(Reproduced with kind permission of David J. Richardson)

A PRESENT DAY view of the Central Library and Graves Art Gallery. Diagonally opposite the western corner of the Central Library building on the opposite side of Surrey Street, facing Tudor Square, is one of Sheffield's newest attractions, the Winter Garden, by Pringle Richards Sharratt. Opened in December 2002, it is linked to the Millennium Galleries (1995–2001) by the same architects. It is the crowning glory of the £120 million 'Heart of the City' project.

THE LYCEUM THEATRE

THIS VIEW, TAKEN in 1937, shows the corner of the Lyceum Theatre and the burnt out shell of the Theatre Royal. The Lyceum Theatre was built on the site of the City Theatre and Circus.

which burned down in 1893. Originally opened as the City Theatre later that same year, designed by Walter Emden with Holmes & Watson, it was substantially remodelled by the architect W.G.R. Sprague (1865–1933), who was responsible for creating some of the most beautiful theatres in London, including Wyndham's and The New Theatre. Surprisingly, although Sprague has more theatres still standing in London than any other architect, Sheffield's Lyceum Theatre is his only remaining theatre outside the capital. During the '70s and '80s it was used mostly for bingo, but in 1989 work commenced on the restoration of this glorious theatre and the complete rebuilding of the backstage area. The historic Theatre Royal opened in 1773 and was altered several times, having been almost completely rebuilt in 1855, with further alterations being carried out in 1901 by Frank Matcham. The disastrous fire which rendered the Theatre Royal beyond repair occurred on 30 December 1935.
(Reproduced with kind permission of David J. Richardson)

THE PHOTOGRAPH ABOVE, taken in 2011 from the same spot across Tudor Square, on the site once occupied by the Theatre Royal, shows Sheffield's famous repertory theatre, the Crucible Theatre, on the right. The round tower-like glass building is Crucible Corner, a recently-built bar and restaurant at 101 Norfolk Street, attached to the Ruskin Building, which replaced catering facilities that used to be in the Crucible Theatre itself.

NORFOLK STREET,
WEST SIDE

THE WEST SIDE of Norfolk Street in 1910 (left). The building in the right foreground is St Marie's Presbytery. The Surrey Street corner of the town hall can be seen at the end of the street.
(Reproduced with kind permission of David J. Richardson)

A SIMILAR VIEW of the west side of Norfolk Street (above) in January 2011, adjusted to include a glimpse of the Cathedral Church of St Marie. Abacus House, 24–26 Norfolk Row, is occupied by a branch of the Coventry Building Society. By no means unappealing, it is one of the least remarkable buildings in the immediate vicinity, which contains some good eighteenth- and early nineteenth-century houses (now offices) as well as Upper Chapel, Sheffield's oldest Noncomformist chapel, parts of which date from 1700. Before the Reformation, the faithful of Sheffield worshipped at the parish church, but by 1570 the Roman Catholic faith was outlawed and kept alive only in isolated places. Before the first Catholic Relief Act in 1778, Catholics in Sheffield met for worship in a room in the Lord's House, home of the Duke of Norfolk's steward for Sheffield in Fargate, until a small chapel was erected at the back of the house in 1812. By 1845 the chapel had become too small and the foundation stone for the present church was laid on 25 March 1847. Designed by Sheffield architect M.E. Hadfield, in the Decorated Gothic style and occupying the site of the chapel of 1812 and its graveyard, St Marie's opened for worship on 11 September 1850. When the new Diocese of Hallam was created in 1980, St Marie's was chosen as the cathedral church.

NORFOLK STREET, EAST SIDE

A VIEW OF the east side of Norfolk Street (opposite), taken in 1933. Hay's Tobacconist, Ye Olde Original Snuff Shoppe, is celebrating family ownership of the shop for 100 years. The shop backs onto properties fronting in Sycamore Street.
(David J. Richardson Collection)

SHEFFIELD'S WORLD FAMOUS Crucible Theatre occupies the site of Hay's Tobacconist today. Some extremely fine theatrical productions have been staged here since the theatre opened in 1971. The theatre has become well known to a wider television audience, as since 1977 the annual World Snooker Championship has been held there. The stage door is located in Norfolk Street, on the extreme left beneath the projecting upper level.

SYCAMORE STREET

SYCAMORE STREET, 1930 (left), shown from its junction with Arundel Street, is one of Sheffield's vanished commercial areas. Part of the Electro Works building can be seen on the right. Sycamore Street ran parallel to Norfolk Street.
(Reproduced with kind permission of David J. Richardson)

THE SITE OF Sycamore Street in January 2011 (above). The right-hand side of the building occupies the site where the Electro Works building once stood, and the glazed portion of the building, which has 'CRUCIBLE' emblazoned across it, roughly marks the width of the old road. The Crucible Theatre was designed by Tanya Moiseiwitsch and the architects Renton Howard Wood Associates were engaged to oversee the work. Construction began in 1969 and continued until 1971, and the theatre opened in November 1971, replacing the Playhouse Repertory Theatre in Townhead Street. A major redevelopment programme of the theatre buildings was completed in 2010. On the left, above the roof of the Crucible Theatre, can be seen the tower of the Methodist's Victoria Hall, situated in Norfolk Street. Built of brick, with stone embellishments in a mixture of Gothic and Arts and Crafts styles, it was designed by Waddington Son & Dunkerley in 1906, with additions carried out in 1908 by W.J. Hale. There is some carved decoration by Alfred and William Tory, including portraits of John and Charles Wesley in the gable.

THE UNIVERSITY OF SHEFFIELD

AN EDWARDIAN POSTCARD view (right) of the
University of Sheffield, taken from Weston Park.
Sir Marcus Samuel Bt (later Lord Bearsted
(1853–1927)), Lord Mayor of London, laid the
foundation stone of the university buildings in 1903.
Constructed to the designs of architect E. Michael Gibbs,

the new Firth Court Building of Sheffield University, on Western Bank, was opened by Their Majesties King Edward VII and Queen Alexandra on 12 July 1905.

THE EDWARDIAN UNIVERSITY of Sheffield building in January 2011 (left), from Weston Park, showing the right-hand elevation of the Firth Court Building in the image above. The building remains substantially the same from the exterior. The statue is of Ebenezer Elliott (1787–1849), the celebrated poet, more commonly known as 'the Corn Law Rhymer', whose poetical works denounced exploitation and oppression of the poor. He was born at Masborough, Rotherham, where his father owned a foundry. Having first worked for his father for seven years for no wages other than a little pocket money, he eventually set up in business for himself and made a successful living in the Sheffield iron trade, later expanding his enterprises to become a steel manufacturer.

THE UNIVERSITY OF SHEFFIELD CONTINUED

THE UNIVERSITY OF Sheffield, *c.*1914 (right). The octagonal Edgar Allen Library on the left, like the other university buildings seen here, was also designed by architect E. Michael Gibbs and added in 1909–11. The university developed from three local institutions: the Sheffield School of Medicine, Firth College and the Sheffield Technical School.

THE ORIGINAL SHEFFIELD University building in 2011 (left). The university had started life as a university college in 1897. The commitment to gain full university status gathered momentum when it was hinted that the University College of Leeds might become the University of Yorkshire. Since those early days the University of Sheffield has grown to become a leading research university. It is a member of the Russell Group of leading research intensive universities. It was ranked 40th in the World's top 100 universities by the Global University Ranking Study in 2009. To date the University of Sheffield has produced five Nobel Prize winners.

MAPPIN ART GALLERY

THE MAPPIN ART Gallery, Weston Park, in a Valentine's postcard view *c*.1900 (right). Weston Park, in which the museum and art gallery are located, was created from the grounds of Weston Hall, built in the early nineteenth century by eminent Sheffield sawmaker Thomas Harrison. On his death, Weston Hall passed to his two spinster daughters and after their deaths it was purchased by Sheffield Corporation for £15,750. Robert Marnock was commissioned to design the park in 1873. The gallery was built at a cost of £15,000 between 1886 and 1888, to the designs of architects Flockton & Gibbs, and linked to the museum. It was

founded under the terms of the will of John Newton Mappin (1800–84), a wealthy cutlery manufacturer, who bequeathed 153 paintings on condition that an art gallery was built to house them. His nephew, Sir Frederick Mappin Bt (1821–1910), presented a further forty-eight pictures, and other bequests followed.

THE MAPPIN ART Gallery in 2011 (left). The building suffered severe bomb damage during the Sheffield Blitz in December 1940, with only the principal façade surviving intact. It now forms part of Weston Park Museum, the component parts of which were named the Sheffield City Museum and Mappin Art Gallery respectively until 2006.

Other titles published by The History Press

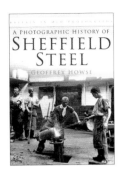

A Photographic History of Sheffield Steel

GEOFFREY HOWSE

Sheffield has built its worldwide reputation on steelmaking. For centuries the city's name was synonymous with steel and today 'made in Sheffield' still guarantees the highest quality. In *A Photographic History of Sheffield Steel*, author Geoffrey Howse has chosen a wide cross-section of photographs of steel and cutlery production in and around the city, primarily from the fascinating collections at Kelham Island Museum.

978 0 7524 5985 1

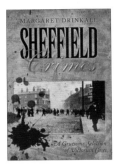

Sheffield Crimes: A Gruesome Selection of Victorian Cases

MARGARET DRINKALL

This volume collects together the most shocking criminal cases from Sheffield's Victorian newspapers. These grisly cases will transport the reader back to a time where horse-drawn carriages clattered through the streets of the city, and the town's gin palaces teemed with thieves, drunkards and fallen women. In an age where the gap between rich and poor was enormous, crime was understandably rife – and the penalties for it dreadful.

978 0 7524 5820 5

Great War Britain Sheffield

TIM LYNCH

An intimate portrayal of Sheffield under the shadow of the Great War, including the tale of a Boy Scout leader's journey to Gallipoli, the terror of the first air raids, and the university's best and brightest who formed their own Pals battalion only to lose poets, writers and students on the Somme. This beautifully illustrated volume contrasts the strikes and political unrest with patriotism and sacrifice in the city they called 'the armourer to the Empire'.

978 0 7509 6048 9

The Little Book of Yorkshire

GEOFFREY HOWSE

The Little Book of Yorkshire is a fascinating, fact-packed compendium of the sort of information which no-one will want to be without. The county's most eccentric inhabitants, famous sons and daughters, royal connections and literally hundreds of intriguing facts about Yorkshire's landscape, cities, towns and villages come together to make one handy, pocket-sized treasure trove of trivia. A remarkably engaging little book, this is essential reading for visitors and locals alike.

978 0 7524 5773 4

Visit our website and discover thousands of other History Press books.

www.thehistorypress.co.uk